LEGO

JURASSIC WORLD

JURASSIC WORLD

COMPLETE DINOSAURIA

LEGO

JURASSIC WORLD

JURASSIC WORLD

COMPLETE DINOSAURIA

if found, return to A

INGEN LABORATORIES

VELOCIRAPTOR

Carnivorous dinosaurs, with long claws and sharp teeth. Very fast and agile, hunt in packs. It is advised to take extra care during an encounter.

I still feel shivers running down my spine when I remember my first meeting with them, even though I'm a gutsy girl!

LAB CARD

STATISTICS

SIZE:	■■■□□
STRENGTH:	■■■□□
SPEED:	■■■■□
ATTACK:	■■■■■
INTELLIGENCE:	■■■■■

They aren't too big . . . but I'd still take care.

I'd give a 4!

It's true, but I wouldn't play chess with them . . . they could bite my hand!

ENVIRONMENT:

Need to be kept in a compound containing stretches of grassy plain and access to water, e.g. small lake. Bushy terrain doesn't bother them.

The main problem is that they can find their way out really quickly!

CHARACTERISTICS:

Clever and cunning predator. Individual animals work together during a hunt.

And they are sooo good at it! When I met them for the first time, I barely made it out alive!

OPERATIONAL COMMENTS:

Very interesting animals. It is suggested to continue observation and attempts at training.

Some people, like Owen Grady (THE Owen Grady!), try to bond with and train them!

1754/67X

INGEN LABORATORIES

VELOCIRAPTOR

OBSERVATIONS:

Raptors have strong hind legs that allow them to run incredibly fast! The legs help with effective hunting and fighting, thanks to a special claw on each paw.

A large, recurved claw on each hind foot can be used as a weapon, to both attack the prey and to protect the raptor. All of the claws are as sharp as a knife.

LAB CARD

Each individual *Velociraptor* has its own distinctive features, such as subtle differences in color, size, and character!

Velociraptors sometimes remind me of lions. Their habitat looks similar too!

Velociraptors live in packs, which helps them hunt for bigger prey and stay safe. They are very social: they basically live, hunt, and protect each other in families, like some modern-day predators.

These dinosaurs care very much for their younglings. They will protect the eggs no matter what—even if it means they have to fight with a very angry *T. rex*! Baby raptors are also usually looked after by older individuals (not only their parents).

VELOCIRAPTOR

Velociraptors can also bond with humans. But don't be fooled! They won't just simply listen to people and be controlled. The relationship has to be based on mutual respect.

They need time to start trusting any human, but I guess it's worth trying.

DO NOT FORGET!

These dinosaurs are incredibly smart. They can cooperate with each other and not only create ambushes, but also organize whole traps for their prey.

I've noticed that their communication patterns play a great role in hunting in a herd. The dinosaurs use various calls: from very subtle to very loud growls.

When trained, they can react to signals made with a clicker. Don't play with a ballpoint pen near them—who knows what they might understand from your clicking!

They always look so impressive!

NOTES:

1754/69X

INGEN LABORATORIES

BLUE

Blue is one of the most extraordinary *Velociraptors* genetically engineered in modern times—she can show not only affection and empathy, but also make conscious decisions. She is a leader of her pack.

Blue is exceptionally intelligent! She is also very loyal.

LAB CARD

Blue is over 12 feet long and almost 6 feet tall—she is almost as tall as her trainer. But her body is much heavier! She weighs around 500 lbs (almost as much as a horse!).

But I wouldn't ever try to ride her!

Since she is a *Velociraptor*, she prefers to stay in overgrown areas with an access to water. She lives with her pack, but her intelligence lets her deal with anything on her own when needed.

Since she is very social, she prefers staying with her pack and with her trainer. She can communicate with Owen Grady by responding to his clicker—so impressive!

1765/30X

BLUE

Her jaws are strong for catching prey!

Since she's a raptor, Blue can run really fast!

Blue has bluish-gray coloration with one stripe on each of her sides, one starting at the eye and the other just below it.

Blue is very good at communicating with both humans and other dinosaurs, supposedly not only with raptors. Her intelligence is impressive!

Apart from being smart, she is also really strong and—like any other raptor—very fast. Her hind legs allow her to run with an immense speed. They also help her with hunting, thanks to the large, recurved claw on each foot.

Even though she was raised by humans and lived with them, and even though she has some friends among them, I would recommend staying away from this dinosaur. Blue may have extraordinary intelligence and emotions, but she is still a representative of a species known for its aggression.

And she still has very sharp teeth and claws!

BLUE

In her own pack, she is a leader of Charlie, Delta, and Echo (other raptors that hatched at the same time as she did). Gaining leadership required fighting with Echo, but now they seem to get along. She is an alpha raptor—and accepts Owen Grady as her alpha human!

Blue is an impressive example of her species, and the fact that she can bond with Owen makes her even more special!

I'd love to meet her, but to be honest ... I'd rather avoid encountering her by chance in her natural habitat with no other humans around!

NOTES:

1765/32X

ATROCIRAPTOR

Fast, medium-sized dinosaur, always ready to attack. The modern ones are trained to hunt on command of their alpha human. Extremely dangerous.

Genetically modified *Atrociraptors* are bigger than their historical versions—and much scarier thanks to it!

These claws would be a threat in their original size, but this big? Oh, they are made to slice everything!

Some of them are quite unique! Just take a look at Ghost! He is even more fearsome thanks to his white-with-reddish-stripes coloration!

All individuals vary in coloration, size, character, etc.

ENVIRONMENT:

They are very much like *Velociraptors*, and they prefer similar, grassy habitats.

CHARACTERISTICS:

Taller than an adult human, slim and sleek, with strong hind legs.

OPERATIONAL COMMENTS:

Atrociraptors always go in packs, ready to surround the prey. They don't stop the chase until they captured their target or it (rarely) finds a way to elude them.

1756/45X

INGEN LABORATORIES

ATROCIRAPTOR

OBSERVATIONS:

They are extremely aggressive and smart! In fact, they have been modified to be larger, faster and more dangerous than any other raptor—and to follow the commands of their alpha human.

The ones you may encounter now are supposed to attack on command of anyone in charge of them. They are great hunters, without a doubt!

They will try to aggressively pursue anything pointed out to them with a red laser beam! I would recommend not getting in the way of anyone who controls the pack!

LAB CARD

They prefer to stay in the wilderness, but can easily find their way even in a busy city. But I really hope no one ever meets them there!

NOTES:

STATISTICS

SIZE:	■ ■ ■ □ □
STRENGTH:	■ ■ ■ ■ □
SPEED:	■ ■ ■ ■ ■
ATTACK:	■ ■ ■ ■ □
INTELLIGENCE:	■ ■ ■ ■ ■

There's no messing with them!

1756/46X

OWEN GRADY

Owen Grady is such an impressive person! His knowledge of modern-day animals is amazing, and when it comes to dinosaurs ... he knows how to deal with them!

He may not be a paleontologist, but he sure knows a lot about dinosaurs!

As an animal behaviorist, Owen was a perfect person to train *Velociraptors*. These raptors are incredibly smart, but training them requires something more than wit: being ready to respect them and create a bond with a herd!

His care and bond with dinosaurs is unique. I always look up to him when it comes to treating them all as feeling and thinking creatures. And, well, I also admire that he is great at surviving every encounter! Dealing with even the fiercest of them comes to him naturally.

Owen's adventures are so inspiring! I have met many dinosaurs, but I would never try to meet some of them THIS CLOSE!

And tricking them to follow his plan? I mean, it is what any person dealing with them would wish to do! Especially when you are trying to keep yourself and others alive!

I wouldn't try this!

INGEN LABORATORIES

GIGANOTOSAURUS

The largest known terrestrial carnivore—measuring around 15 feet tall, 42 feet long, with a sharp backbone and strong hind legs that allow him to run incredibly fast.

Yes, he is a boy ... a really BIG one!

LAB CARD

ENVIRONMENT:

He prefers any place on land where he can find prey big enough to satisfy his appetite.

CHARACTERISTICS:

Enormous (as tall as the tallest giraffes!), weighing up to 7 tons. He mostly eats other large dinosaur species.

But I'm sure he can also eat a truck full of baked chicken drumsticks all at once, and be happy about it!

OPERATIONAL COMMENTS:

Giganotosaurus is smart enough to know that there is no point in losing energy by hunting for fun. He is moderately aggressive and hunts mostly for food.

1757/21X

He is a threat even to the mighty *Tyrannosaurus rex*—it is not surprising, considering their sizes!!!

GIGANOTOSAURUS

OBSERVATIONS:

He is the biggest genetically engineered terrestrial carnivore dinosaur! He is even bigger than *T. rex*. This giant can be surprisingly sneaky: his colors serve as camouflage and help him hide in overgrown areas!

Two-clawed front arms are rather small compared to the rest of his body. He can't even scratch his own nose with them when it's itchy!

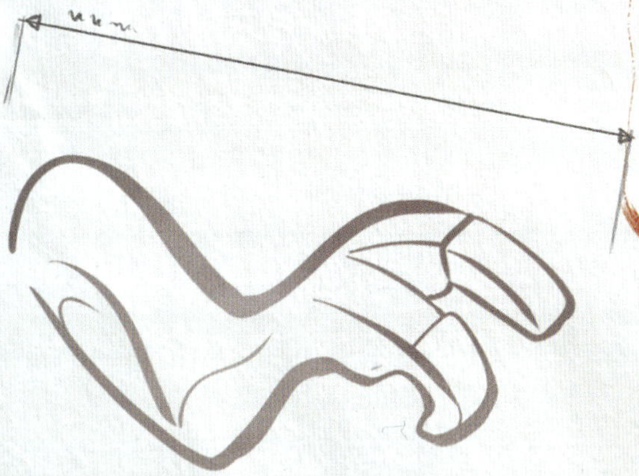

A dinosaur this big needs a lot of meat to fill his stomach—and he doesn't like being hungry.

LAB CARD

His teeth are very much like the ones of modern crocodiles, just bigger. They are made to rip the food apart, but not to chew.

1757/22X

GIGANOTOSAURUS

Avoid running away from him—hiding is a better idea.

This dinosaur is a singular representative of his species! An incredibly unique character!
I always wonder if they would cooperate with each other if there were more than one *Giganotosaurus* ...

But let's not check, one is more than enough!

STATISTICS

SIZE:	■■■■■
STRENGTH:	■■■■■
SPEED:	■■■■□
ATTACK:	■■■□□
INTELLIGENCE:	■■■□□

It should be a 6!

He is well-aware of his own skills.

NOTES:

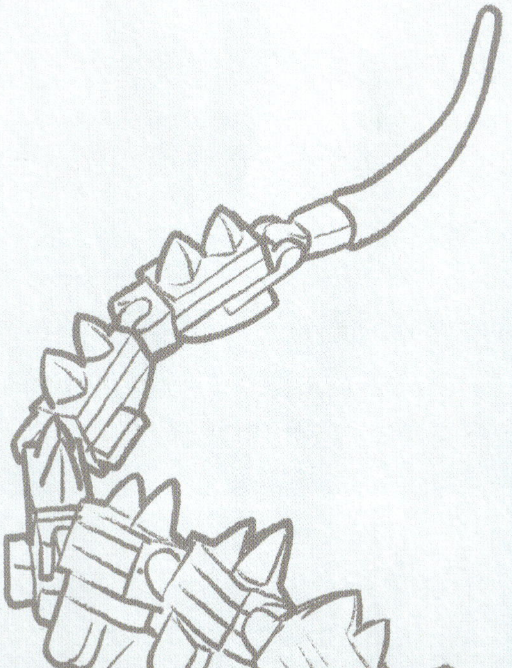

1757/23X

MOSASAURUS

The largest carnivore of Jurassic World, aquatic, ready to eat anything that happens to be close enough. Hunts for food the size of great white sharks.

If you think about it, she is a perfect "sea dragon" for a pirate story! Snapping on ships is something she is VERY capable of.

She is grayish-blue with a creamy underbelly. This coloration makes her harder to notice in the deep waters.

The one biologically engineered for Jurassic World is female!

ENVIRONMENT:

This dinosaur lives in waters deep enough for her, hunting in the top parts of the reservoir (and sometimes reaches out to the shore).

As long as seven polar bears! Or five African elephants! Or two school buses!

CHARACTERISTICS:

Over 70 feet long, with enormous jaws ready to snap at any prey (upon which she sneaks up unnoticed).

OPERATIONAL COMMENTS:

Unable to chew, she has to swallow her food whole. Sometimes her teeth help her rip it into pieces (but most fish are just smaller than her individual teeth).

1758/91X

OBSERVATIONS:

Since there is only one *Mosasaurus*, she lives a solitary life. Having no one to communicate with, she apparently has no need for vocalization. The only sounds she has currently been heard to produce are the splashes she makes when emerging from and falling back into water.

It can be really hard to find any company for such a giant—but I've heard that she has been seen peacefully mingling with a pod of humpback whales. They are the closest in size to her among modern-day animals.

Can you imagine that she is related to Komodo Dragons? She is just a bit bigger. Like, seven times bigger.

LAB CARD

1758/92X

MOSASAURUS

When she was locked in her pool, she didn't seem interested in eating the visitors who were watching her from the edges of the tank. In the wild, she willingly catches anything that comes to the shore close enough to the water.

Can eat LITERALLY ANYTHING foolish enough to wander too close to the water's edge!

There is no hope to outrun her with a boat, and don't even think about just swimming away—the best thing to do with the *Mosasaurus* is avoiding her.

LAB CARD

STATISTICS

I'd give it a 7 out of 5, to be honest!

SIZE:	■■■■■
STRENGTH:	■■■■■
SPEED:	■■■■□
ATTACK:	■■■■□
INTELLIGENCE:	■■■□□

← She is SNEAKY!

NOTES:

1758/93X

STEGOSAURUS

Big herbivores with backs full of 2-feet tall spikes. These dinosaurs feed on low-growing plants (ferns are their favorite).

Over 30 feet long, almost 17 feet tall, and heavier than two rhinos! *Stegosaurus* are like road rollers in the jungle!

LAB CARD

This amount of meat would be a great catch for any predator, but getting through the spikes makes it much less desirable!

ENVIRONMENT:

They prefer staying in the open plains, but can also be seen moving slowly through forests, nonchalantly eating their favorite food.

CHARACTERISTICS:

Heavy body, massive legs and tiny head. *Stegosauruses* are said to be low on intelligence—they have exceptionally small brains.

The size of a kitten! Compared to them being as big as an elephant. That IS a tiny brain.

OPERATIONAL COMMENTS:

These dinosaurs live in family groups and herds. They are protective of their babies, but they would prefer to be left alone rather than fight.

STEGOSAURUS

OBSERVATIONS:

They really don't like loud noises and find them extremely alarming. If you want a *Stegosaurus* to withdraw from a certain place, using air horns, whistles, etc. can be helpful. The dinosaur will probably just back off—high-pitched sounds are not something this species likes.

Who does, honestly?

Encountering them can be dangerous only if you get in the way of their tail. It can be swung really fast—easily knocking down big trees and piercing metal with the spikes.

Just be careful around them!

The research on this species is so fascinating! Especially figuring out what these spikes are for ...

STATISTICS

SIZE:	■■■■□
STRENGTH:	■■■□□
SPEED:	■■□□□
ATTACK:	■■□□□
INTELLIGENCE:	■□□□□

They are similar in size to an elephant.

Well, the tail alone is a solid 4 out of 5.

NOTES:

TO DO:

get some more photos of Stegosaurus for my research!

1769/42X

CLAIRE DEARING

Claire Dearing is a real leader! She is so cool and smart, and knows how to deal with almost anything!

Claire is an Operations Manager at Jurassic World—and she really does her best to make sure that the park functions properly and that guests are satisfied with their visit.

She cares about her job very much, and I am really not surprised at all! I mean, who wouldn't want to work with all those dinosaurs around?

Claire knows her way around! She is very bright and always knows what to say. She cares about justice for both humans and dinosaurs.

It takes a lot of courage to deal with all those dinosaurs and all the people around them! Claire is really good at that.

I admire the fact that she is so good at admitting she was wrong—for a while she was too business-oriented, but she realized that she should focus more on the welfare of the dinosaurs. It takes a lot of guts to accept your own mistakes and a lot to tell it to others! She also knows when to ask for help—and when to help others.

1763/56X

INGEN LABORATORIES

TRICERATOPS

Massive and strong, this dinosaur lives in herds. Acts similar to bison. When approached, can be dangerous.

They may be herbivores, but I would still avoid getting too close to them—especially when they are in a bad mood.

LAB CARD

Did you know that *Triceratops* has always been Alan Grant's favorite dinosaur?

If searching for fossils and studying them used to be exciting enough, I can only imagine how emotional it was for Dr. Grant to meet the genetically engineered version at Jurassic World!

These creatures are really beautiful! And their size is so impressive!

ENVIRONMENT:

They live on scrubby grasslands. You can locate their territory easily: they leave roughly circular clearings in the fighting spots.

They also leave enormous piles of poo all around ...

CHARACTERISTICS:

Heavy, sturdy, with thick skin. They can be easily recognized because of the unique huge crowns and triple-horns on their heads.

OPERATIONAL COMMENTS:

They always protect the herd—especially the young ones—very well. They can even stand up to a *T. rex*.

And chase her away with their massive horns!

1759/11X

INGEN LABORATORIES

They like any territory with enough plants to satisfy their stomachs (theme park full of concrete doesn't sound good).

TRICERATOPS

These horns are MASSIVE!

Their head makes up to 1/3 of their body length!

Unlike their historical counterpart, they don't have claws.

Their massive legs are a bit elephant-like.

LAB CARD

OBSERVATIONS:

Triceratops are not too intelligent. They rely on their herd when it comes to making decisions.

When you approach them, remember that they are not aggressive, but their size and strength can be dangerous. Usually they will just ignore you—unless you bother them too much. They don't back down from confrontation if needed, and just like a bothered cow, they can kick you or use their heads to bump you.

Just remember they are "slightly" stronger than cows.

STATISTICS

SIZE:	■■■■□
STRENGTH:	■■■■□
SPEED:	■■■□□
ATTACK:	■■■□□
INTELLIGENCE:	■□□□□

Triceratops are a lot like cows!

1759/12X

TRICERATOPS

These dinosaurs are known for their massive, "armored" heads. The horns and bony frills serve as both helmet and weapon when *Triceratops* is being attacked by any predator—or by one of its own species.

Every fight leaves visible scratches on the sides of their bony frills. Some scars look really ... well, scary.

They really care about their hatchlings! The herd is very protective of the adorable little ones.

I don't blame people for wanting to pet them, but I won't stop repeating:
DO NOT TOUCH ANY *TRICERATOPS*!

They eat both soft and tough plants, snapping them with their beaks and teeth (that act as enormous pairs of scissors). Since *Triceratops* are not the smartest ones around, they sometimes eat something inedible.

LAB CARD

Triceratops communicate with each other using a mix of bellows and snorts.

Can be hard when they have a cold and their noses are stuffed!

NOTES:

1759/13X

INGEN LABORATORIES

PTERANODON

Big flying reptiles, living in flocks, roosting and nesting on cliffsides. They mostly eat fish, swallowing them whole.

LAB CARD

ENVIRONMENT:

They build their nests mainly on cliffs and on hill sides, high enough to be able to quickly spot their prey and to protect their eggs from other predators.

25 feet would be around 5 park benches long!

CHARACTERISTICS:

These reptiles are really big, with wing span around 25 feet. They tend to attack with claws and beaks. They live in flocks.

OPERATIONAL COMMENTS:

Look out for them when flying, especially when approaching potential nesting sites.

They look amazing when flying! For them, what is really amazing are helicopters! They always want to take a closer look at them ... making landing anything but easy.

1760/04X

PTERANODON

OBSERVATIONS:

Pteranodons don't really attack people, but they will if provoked or simply bothered too much.
Since they are irritated by loud noises, you can try to scare them away, but better just look for a hiding spot.

If you ever happen to encounter them too closely, be very careful!

The beaks are very sharp—which is quite important, since *Pteranodons* do not have any teeth.
They catch their favorite food—fish—by diving into water and snapping them up.
It's worth it to get wet for a really big fish!

Pteranodons communicate by screeching and squawking—not really pleasant sounds, if you ask me!

STATISTICS

SIZE:	■■■■□
STRENGTH:	■■■□□
SPEED:	■■■■□
ATTACK:	■■■■□ ← They can be surprisingly sneaky!
INTELLIGENCE:	■■■□□

↑ But really observative!!!

Pteranodons are social creatures, living in flocks, nesting together and protecting their young ones. They are very protective of their eggs and hatchlings—parents will surely try to defend their nests if anybody disturbs them.

Don't ever touch the eggs or small *Pteranodons* found in the wild, even if they seem friendly or cute!

1760/05X

PTERANODON

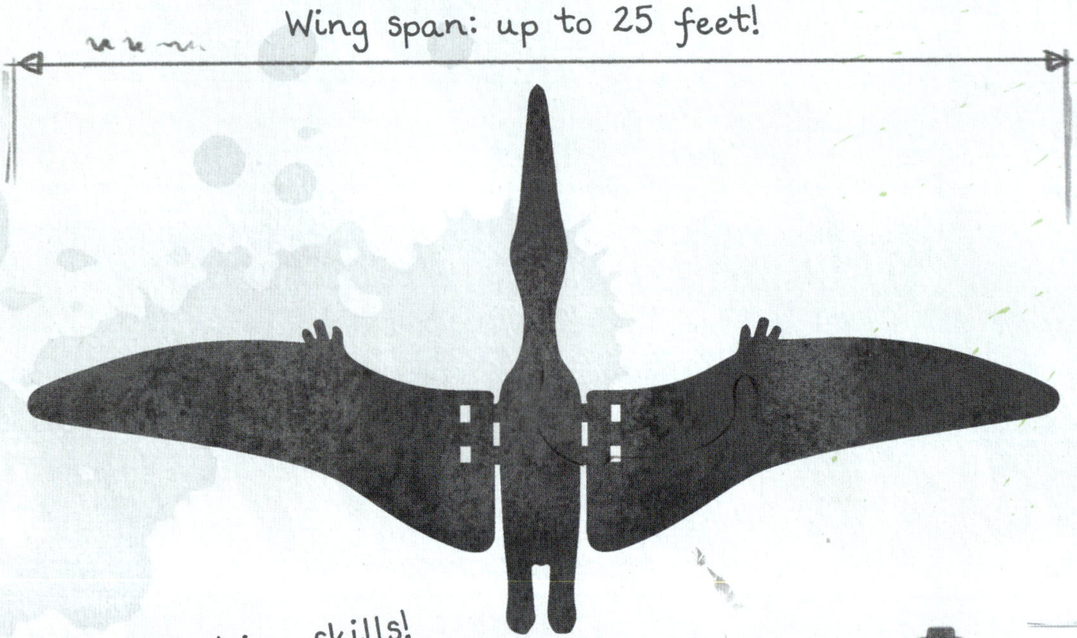

Remarkable fishing skills! Unfortunately, they usually eat their catch before anyone can take a commemorative photo! That was a lucky shot!

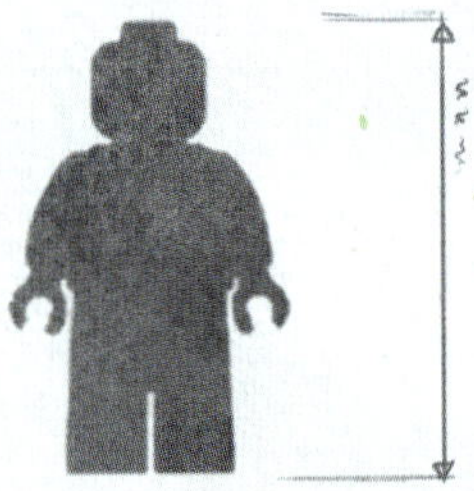

Males tend to have more colorful and ornate crests than females, which makes it easy to tell them apart.

But both males and females are just as dangerous and smart.

No need to tell them apart to know that you should avoid interactions!

NOTES:

1760/06X

QUETZALCOATLUS

Big pterosaurs with sharp, reinforced beaks, ready to pin anything down. They are solitary, can be seen flying on long journeys alone.

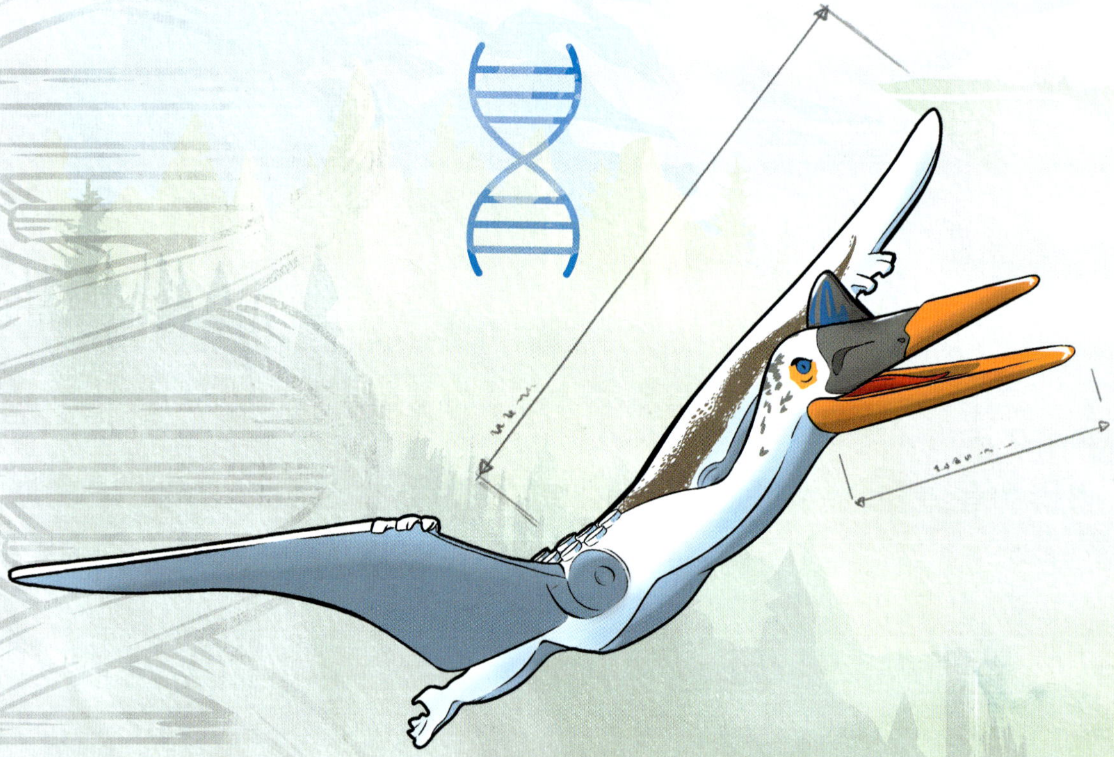

They are a bit similar to *Pteranodons*, but they nest and move alone, not in flocks. They are also much bigger!

LAB CARD

They wouldn't nest here, but can be spotted catching prey near a river!

ENVIRONMENT:

They build extremely large nests for their eggs and hatchlings high above the ground (on towers, hills, etc.).

CHARACTERISTICS:

One of the biggest flying animals of all time, their wing span allows them to fly across continents and even around the world, catching the right air currents.

OPERATIONAL COMMENTS:

Avoid getting close to their nests—they have strong instincts when it comes to taking care of their hatchlings.

1762/73X

OBSERVATIONS:

Even though they are not very sociable, they sometimes have to communicate among each other. They do it by making deep, booming calls that are extremely loud.

Can you imagine an animal this big flying? They really make the earth tremble when they land!

LAB CARD

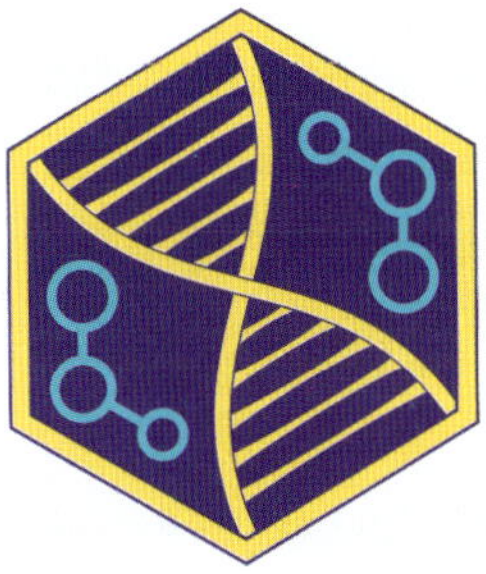

Genetically engineered dinosaurs and pterosaurs are a great achievement of modern science! The DNA sequences from fossils are usually incomplete—and filling them can be tricky.

These pterosaurs have an appetite as big as them: they can eat almost everything (both plants and animals—they are omnivores).

Because they don't have teeth, they usually take the food apart with their sharp beaks or swallow it in one bite. They aren't very picky when it comes to food, but the bigger the better!

When grounded and standing on their wings, the *Quetzalcoatlus* tower over dinosaurs as large as the *T. rex*! They can measure up to almost 16 feet high (from head to feet, standing on the ground) and almost 30 feet long (from beak to tail), and their wings can have a span of 36 feet! What a giant!

1762/74X

QUETZALCOATLUS

Catching the right air current can take them to another continent in one journey!

Quetzalcoatlus was named after the Aztec feathered serpent god. And the name quite fits this pterosaur!

When it comes to being "feathered serpents" ... well, they are not serpents, but they ARE reptiles. And feathers? They don't have them—but maybe that is the missing part of the DNA of modern clones!

Their mighty size and strength make them the actual rulers of the sky. They can travel fast to really distant places without getting tired. And the fact they can eat almost anything makes them even more fearsome!

STATISTICS

SIZE:	■■■■■
STRENGTH:	■■■■□
SPEED:	■■■■■ ← When flying, of course!
ATTACK:	■■■□□
INTELLIGENCE:	■■■□□

NOTES:

ELLIE SATTLER

Ellie Sattler is another role model I look up to in my research and when encountering dinosaurs! Her knowledge about prehistoric environments is so impressive!

Ellie is a paleobotanist: she does research on the plants from the past, and she knows her way around any overgrown area!

Ellie is a great woman with a lot of character traits that I admire! She is adventurous, smart, loyal, and she can stand up for herself and others.

Even though her main interest is *flora*, she never stops admiring dinosaurs. She is very empathetic toward them and knows well that these animals have their own needs.

Ellie is always ready to get things done. She doesn't get scared away by anything (well, maybe a *T. rex*) and she always tries to do her best.

I'd love to contact her and learn more about her encounters with dinosaurs! I'm sure she has a lot of stories to tell!

PYRORAPTOR

Terrifying, medium-sized dinosaurs hunting in packs. Not much is known about them—require deeper research.

Look at these colors! These dinosaurs are really breathtaking!

Pyroraptors are great at stalking their prey and hiding from them, even though they are brightly colored! They can hide in any bush and remain really quiet!

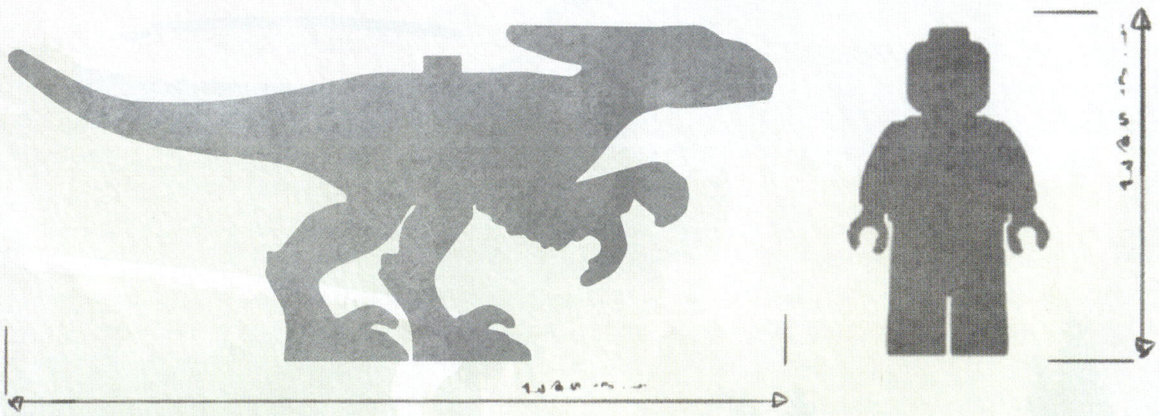

ENVIRONMENT:

They usually hide from the eyesight of humans, but can live in any conditions, from extremely cold to tropical.
Since they are semiaquatic, they can also hunt in water.

CHARACTERISTICS:

Covered with brightly-colored feathers that aid their mobility and insulate them against even the most extreme temperature conditions.

OPERATIONAL COMMENTS:

Seek shelter if you believe you are close to them: they are extremely aggressive.

1761/19X

PYRORAPTOR

OBSERVATIONS:

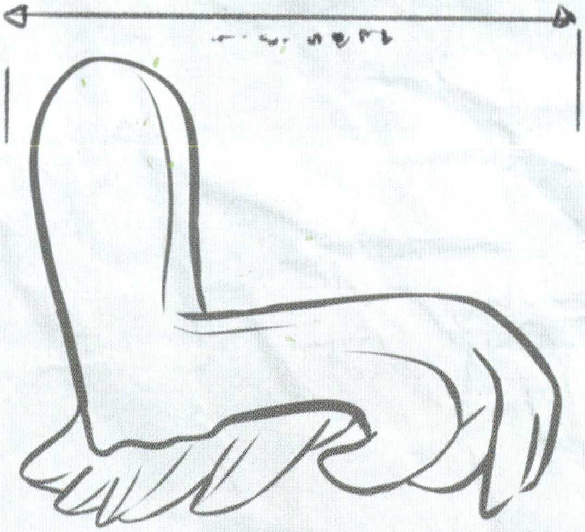

Pyroraptors' colors are really bright—they look like a running fire! They live up to their name: *Pyroraptor* means "the fire thief."

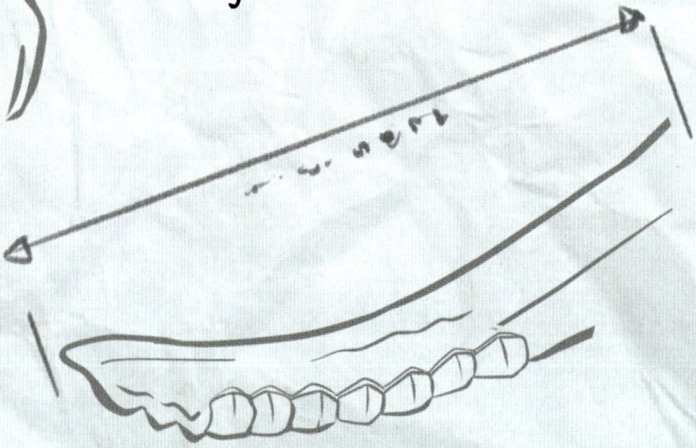

It has not yet been researched whether they are immune to fire, but extreme weather is not a big deal for these dinosaurs.

Taking this photo was a part of a really dangerous adventure! Note for future encounters: turn the camera's flash off!!!

Pyroraptors usually live in small packs. They can cooperate when hunting for a bigger prey (even much bigger than them!), ambushing and attacking together.

But if they happen to be alone, they can be satisfied eating smaller reptiles, mammals, and even fish! They are surprisingly good at catching prey underwater.

1761/20X

PYRORAPTOR

When hunting, they mostly use their teeth and front claws. Additionally, each hind leg of this dinosaur has one enlarged curved claw, perfect for pinning down prey.

Since these dinosaurs are really hard to encounter, it's slowly getting frustrating to observe them! I won't give up, though!

STATISTICS

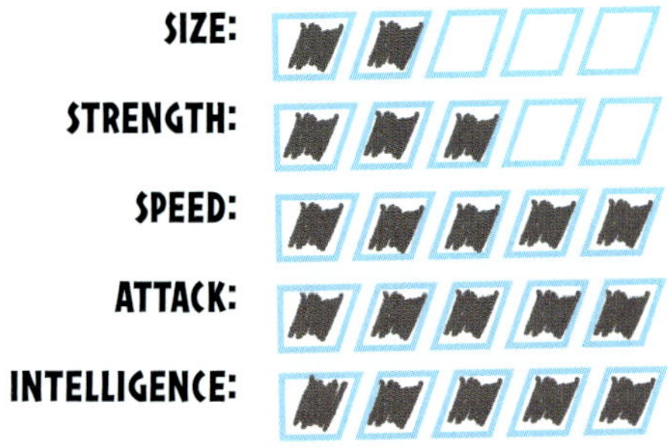

Just avoid them if you are not currently researching this species.

They can often outsmart humans . . .

There is so much more to learn about them ...

NOTES:

INGEN LABORATORIES

TYRANNOSAURUS REX

Ferocious, instinct-driven predators, known for her strong hind legs and being ready to fight. One of the first dinosaurs genetically engineered in modern days.

LAB CARD

Observing a *T. rex* from above is a good idea! She flies as well as she swims.

(And she really doesn't do either well.)

TYRANNOSAURUS REX

ENVIRONMENT:

She stays in overgrown areas, searching for prey and hiding. She feels safe on land.

CHARACTERISTICS:

T. rex is a heavy, big predator, with strong jaws and insatiable appetite.

OPERATIONAL COMMENTS:

She has incredibly sharp instincts, including the parental one—she is ready to protect her potential young fiercely.

She is always ready to rumble, no matter when, where, or with whom!

OBSERVATIONS:

T. rex seems to base her hunting on scents and movement: apparently she doesn't identify prey well when it is standing still right in front of her.

LAB CARD

It's always a good idea to hide when you see a *T. rex* approaching!

STATISTICS

SIZE:	■■■■■
STRENGTH:	■■■■■
SPEED:	■■■■□
ATTACK:	■■■■□
INTELLIGENCE:	■■□□□

Well, the size of a school bus!

Thanks to her hind legs!

I wouldn't judge her so harshly! She is at least 4!

T. rex is one of the most dangerous creatures to ever walk on this planet. Her body is made to hunt and succeed at hunting—no matter what!

In fact, she refuses to go down without a fight—even when the opponent is bigger. But she surely wouldn't be good at boxing with those tiny front paws!

TYRANNOSAURUS REX

NOTES:

Fossils are impressive enough to make you afraid of this dinosaur. Imagine meeting one face to face!

When it comes to hunting, it is quite understandable why this dinosaur is so fierce! *T. rex* requires at least 380 lbs of meat every day—that is a whole big pig!

INGEN LABORATORIES

ANKYLOSAURUS

Big, heavy and covered in osteoderms. *Ankylosaurus*, despite being herbivores, can be dangerous. Their massive tail is like a hammer.

They can become defensive when scared: bright colors and loud noises can be mistaken as threat displays to an Ankylosaurus. Try not to stress them if you want to avoid confrontation.

LAB CARD

ENVIRONMENT:

They live in bushy, overgrown areas with lots of their favorite plants.

They really like to hide between ferns and palm trees! And to eat them.

CHARACTERISTICS:

They are heavy, bulky dinosaurs, known for their osteoderms (bones that have grown into the skin), that create an armor around their whole bodies.

Even their eyelids are protected! Can you imagine?

OPERATIONAL COMMENTS:

Grown-up individuals require over 130 pounds of ferns—their favorite kind of food—a day.

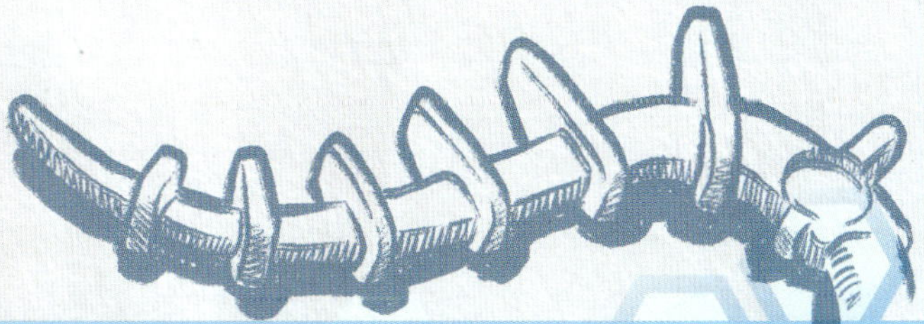

1766/68X

ANKYLOSAURUS

OBSERVATIONS:

They are not really aggressive, but they tend to throw temper tantrums.

These dinosaurs don't hunt, since they are herbivores. Even though they don't hunt for food, they can harm anyone who potentially causes them any threat. Their spikey tails, when swung, can generate over 400 megapascals of force—more than four times the impact stress needed to break a bone. That can easily scare away many predators!

Since almost all of *Ankylosaurus'* bodies are protected, they are basically wearing armor—thick, durable, and covered with sharp spikes! It can provide protection from being eaten by even the most dangerous carnivores.

ANKYLOSAURUS

These dinosaurs live in groups—and communicate between each other using hoots and honks. *Ankylosaurus* can produce these sounds thanks to having complex nasal passages ... so they are basically humming through their nose, just really, really, really loud!

They sometimes remind me of elephants: living in groups, eating plants, and weighing around 8 tons. It was hard to imagine how big they really are before I met them.

Their size makes them even more breathtaking: the adult individuals are almost 12 feet tall and over 30 feet long!

LAB CARD

STATISTICS

SIZE:	■ ■ ■ ■ □
STRENGTH:	■ ■ ■ ■ □
SPEED:	■ ■ □ □ □
ATTACK:	■ ■ □ □ □
INTELLIGENCE:	■ □ □ □ □

Smart enough to find any tasty plant growing close to the ground.

NOTES:

1766/70X

ALAN GRANT

Doctor Grant is someone who doesn't need introduction in the dinosaur world! This renowned paleontologist is surely the person you should look up to if you want to learn about dinosaurs!

His books are great, and his knowledge about dinosaurs is wide! His research was crucial even before he learned about Jurassic World dinosaurs.

I can only imagine how thrilling it was for Dr. Grant to see that objects of his research were alive, walking in front of him ...

I admire not only his research, but also his character! He is brave, intelligent, and takes responsibility for keeping everyone around him safe!

It is easy to understand that meeting face-to-face with *Velociraptors* could have been a traumatic experience even for the bravest scientist!
And I kind of understand that for such an experienced researcher these dinosaurs can seem to be just some theme-park creations ...

But I KNOW Dr. Grant is still in awe of them!

INGEN LABORATORIES

STYGIMOLOCH

Rather small (to medium) for a dinosaur. Their characteristic feature is a powerful dome-shaped skull that can knock down or crash through almost anything. Their necks are protected by the spikes on the back of the head.

Hind legs of Stygimolochs are very strong!

LAB CARD

ENVIRONMENT:

They feed on deep roots—and are always searching for areas covered in trees and other big plants.

They tend to damage all the big flora around them. (Unfortunately, even on cultivated land.)

CHARACTERISTICS:

Slim, with thickened skull and horns, have small beaks that allow them to effectively rip bite-sized parts off the plants.

They really like ferns and other low-lying soft plants. Better that than roots of orchard trees!

OPERATIONAL COMMENTS:

They smack their heads not only into predators, but also into each other, to fight for a position in a herd.

They are the most aggressive when they are fighting with each other. They can accidentally bump someone by mistake. !!!

1767/80X

INGEN LABORATORIES

STYGIMOLOCH

OBSERVATIONS:

These dinosaurs are quite talkative—they use various sounds to communicate. The sounds themselves are no threat, but you should pay attention to them: the snorts and grunts of *Stygimolochs* can resemble that of small dogs and pigs and attract not only curious humans, but also hungry predators!

Stygimolochs would do their best to protect themselves from much bigger predators, but I don't think they would protect anyone else.

The crown of spikes on the head not only looks extraordinary, but also provides protection against being bitten on the back of the neck.

LAB CARD

STATISTICS

SIZE: ■■■□□

STRENGTH: ■■■□□

SPEED: ■■■■□

ATTACK: ■■■□□

INTELLIGENCE: ■■□□□

The modern ones seem to be bigger than the *Stygimolochs* from the past!

Don't underestimate them!

Stygimolochs don't like fuss or loud sounds! When you encounter them, try to remain quiet. Don't shout, don't whistle, and don't honk at them with your car horn.

But I honestly don't know how they feel about singing.

To keep them calm, avoid approaching them in vehicles. If you want to get closer to a *Stygimoloch*, just walk slowly toward the dinosaur.

They usually live in small groups (sometimes on their own), both on plain terrain with some overgrown bushes and in thick forests. They move quite fast thanks to their strong hind legs.

1767/81X

STYGIMOLOCH

They are not big, but I guarantee they are heavy! You shouldn't try to pick them up ... unless you are a bodybuilder. They weigh over 500 lbs!

They are really easy to recognize: smaller than an adult human, with hardened skulls and spikes on the back of their heads.

Interesting fact: you can identify older individuals by the size of their spikes. They get smaller with age!

LAB CARD

NOTES:

1767/82X

INGEN LABORATORIES

BRACHIOSAURUS

Enormous, exceptionally tall dinosaurs. Live in herds, leaving ground behind them extremely well-worn. Calm and rather slow, they stay safe thanks to the size of their bodies.

LAB CARD

Can you imagine how hard it was to collect all the bones for this enormous neck?!

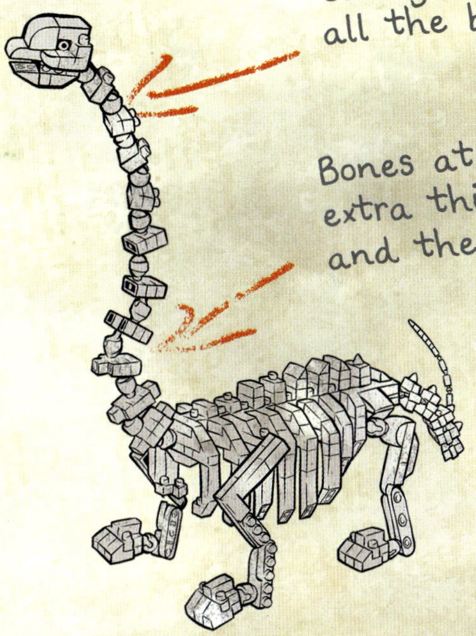

Bones at this spine segment have to be extra thick to keep the rest of the neck and the head steady.

Brachiosaurus' skeleton may seem bulky, but it is vital for the dinosaur to move this massive body!

ENVIRONMENT:

Since they feed on tall trees, chomping on their leaves and branches, they like forested areas with access to water.

What an amazing view to see them eating!

CHARACTERISTICS:

Brachiosaurus have really long necks and heavy, thick legs. These dinosaurs stay in groups, being very social and curious.

OPERATIONAL COMMENTS:

They are huge, but thanks to their coloration and shape, they can hide amongst thickets of tall trees.

. . . maybe by pretending to be a tree on a small hill.

1768/14X

OBSERVATIONS:

Despite being enormous, *Brachiosaurus* do not pose a direct threat to anyone (unless they step on someone by accident). If you have to, approach them slowly. They won't eat you, but still, the best idea is to keep your distance. Falling leftovers from their meals can be really dangerous!

You know what else can be dangerous? Their poop. It is surprisingly heavy when coming from above onto your head ... Trust me.

Since they live in groups, they act like other herd animals: they take care of their younglings, they move together, and they sometimes fight with each other.

But they are usually calm giants.

Their size is their biggest protection—only a starving carnivore would attack a *Brachiosaurus*.

LAB CARD

They are really curious, but not really smart or sneaky. Even when provided with accidental free access beyond their area, they won't escape—unless something startles them. What's the point of running, if the trees are on this side of the fence?

Living in a herd requires some form of communication, and these giants find a proper way to talk to each other. They make deep, resonating calls that can be heard from far away.

To me these sounds are a lot like the songs of a whale. *Brachiosaurus* is a lot like a land-whale with a very long neck, and a pack of friends following everywhere.

1768/15X

BRACHIOSAURUS

These calm giants travel slowly from one point to another, stomping through any terrain, leaving their huge footprints, and eating any plants they can reach with their long necks.

Eating plants growing near the ground can be tricky for a *Brachiosaurus*! It is not easy to lower their necks to the small ferns or bushes.

Thankfully, they can reach the tallest trees and eat leaves from them. These dinosaurs rely on eating foliage that is out of reach for most of the herbivores.

When they eat from trees, they can leave low-growing plants to other dinosaurs ... but they usually leave them trampled on.

LAB CARD

STATISTICS

SIZE:	5 of 5 filled
STRENGTH:	5 of 5 filled
SPEED:	2 of 5 filled
ATTACK:	1 of 5 filled
INTELLIGENCE:	1 of 5 filled

I'd say 6 out of 5.

Especially when they stomp on the ground and shake the earth.

NOTES:

1768/16X

CARNOTAURUS

Tall dinosaurs with tiny forelimbs and small horns. Fast runners with rather weak bite force, satisfied when able to feed on some small prey before *T. rex* decides to hunt for them.

Their hind legs are great for running!
These dinosaurs can outrun a *T. rex*!

ENVIRONMENT:

Prefer areas with bushy *flora*, full of smaller and medium prey. *Carnotaurus* cannot fight bigger predators and they need some places to hide.

CHARACTERISTICS:

Average in size, known for their horns (bull-like: *Carnotaurus* means "meat-eating bull"). These dinosaurs are very fast.

But the proportions of the body are a bit off, making it hard to keep balance while turning. Running away in zigzag patterns is a good idea!

OPERATIONAL COMMENTS:

They are warm-colored: some sport brown and orange coloration, while others have darker contrast, even with pinkish marks.

177/91X

INGEN LABORATORIES

CARNOTAURUS

OBSERVATIONS:

Carnotaurus can be smaller and less aggressive than a *T. rex*, but are still very dangerous predators. They are endurance hunters: they rely on following their prey rather than catching it fast. *Carnotaurus* don't get tired easily, and they are really patient.

Though they enjoy the chase, they also don't mind catching a slow-moving prey. Maybe that's why they eat turtles?

These dinosaurs are easily identified thanks to their horns. They may look like a weapon, but are there mostly for ... decoration. Every single individual in a group of *Carnotaurus* has unique horns, so they also help with identification.

This dinosaur is as big as an adult Asian elephant!

LAB CARD

Hiding between palms and bushes is a good idea.

Look at these tiger-like stripes!

All of the paws have a set of sharp claws!

Taking this photo was risky!

1771/92X

Almost 10 feet tall and 35 feet long, a *Carnotaurus* is big enough to scare away anyone. That is, except the *T. rex*, which is 7 feet taller than the *Carnotaurus*!

Encountering a *Carnotaurus* can be really dangerous. If you want to hide somewhere, choose dense cover (a forest or some rocky terrain) or some sturdy building!

If you decide to run away, remember not to rely only on your legs: setting a trap or using a pit to make them trip is a better idea!

Carnotaurus have really tiny front limbs! But this disproportion doesn't make them any less scary!

LAB CARD

STATISTICS

SIZE:	■■■■□
STRENGTH:	■■■■■
SPEED:	■■■■■
ATTACK:	■■■■■
INTELLIGENCE:	■■■□□

Their hind limbs are slender and strong, helping them run really fast!

NOTES:

1771/92X

BUILDING INSTRUCTIONS

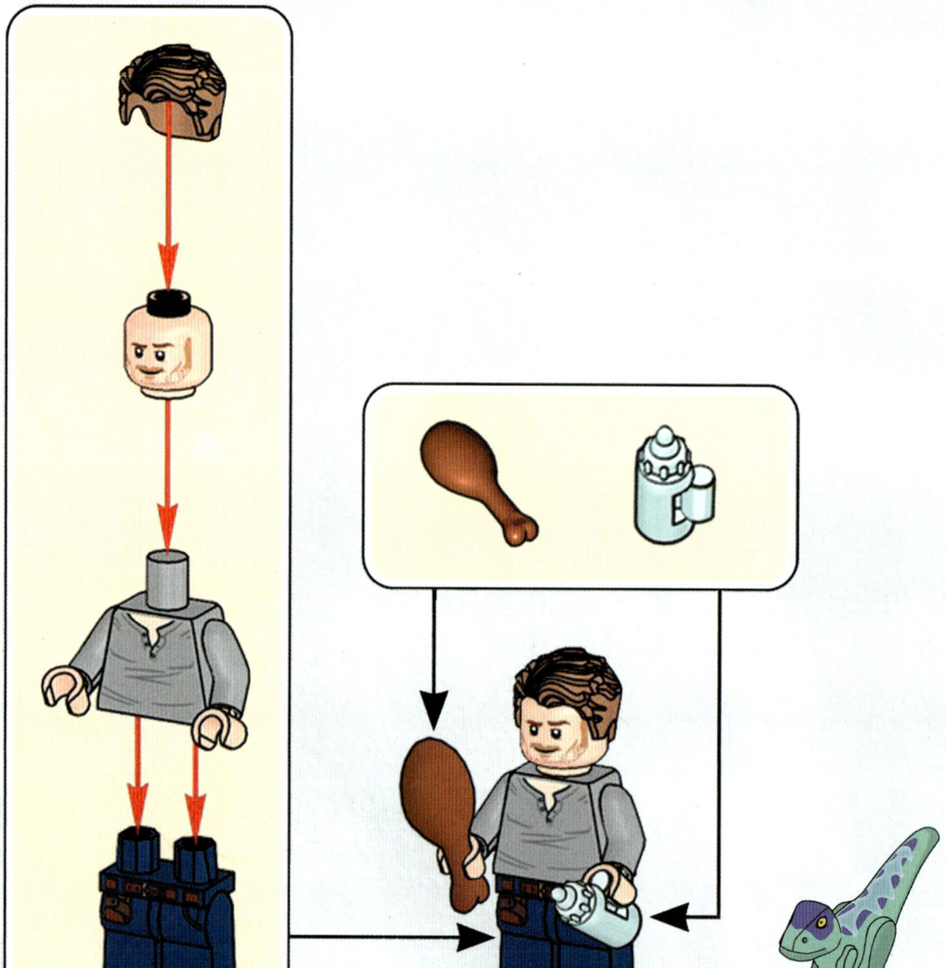

WHO WOULD HAVE THOUGHT THAT THE BOOK WITH THE MOST INFORMATION ABOUT DINOSAURS WOULD BE FOUND ACCIDENTALLY IN SOME BUSHES? THIS AMAZING COMPILATION OF NOTES AND SCIENTIFIC RESEARCH TAKES YOU AS CLOSE AS POSSIBLE TO THE AWESOME DINOSAURS FROM LEGO® JURASSIC WORLD™. BIG AND SMALL, AGGRESSIVE AND CALM, FLYING, RUNNING, AND SWIMMING ... LEARN ABOUT THEM ALL IN THIS COMPLETE DINOSAURIA! BUT WHO IS THE AUTHOR? THAT REMAINS A MYSTERY, BUT IF YOU EVER MEET HER—PLEASE GIVE HER BACK HER NOTES!

Manufactured by AMEET Sp. z o.o.
under license from the LEGO Group.

AMEET Sp. z o.o.
Nowe Sady 6, 94-102 Łódź – Poland
ameet@ameet.eu
www.ameet.eu

Published in the US and Canada by Sourcebooks
1935 Brookdale Road, Suite 139
Naperville, IL 60563
Please keep the Sourcebooks address for future reference.

www.LEGO.com

...nufactured, printed, and assembled in Shenzhen, China

sourcebooks wonderland
sourcebookskids.com

Not for individual sale

6+

MIX
Paper from responsible sources
FSC® C144528